Debating Supreme Court Decisions

New York Times v. Sullivan and the Freedom of the Press Debate

Debating Supreme Court Decisions

Catherine McGlone

Enslow Publishers, Inc.

40 Industrial Road   PO Box 38
Box 398   Aldershot
Berkeley Heights, NJ 07922 Hants GU12 6BP
USA   UK

http://www.enslow.com

For Joe

Library of Congress Cataloging-in-Publication Data

McGlone, Catherine.
    New York Times v. Sullivan and the freedom of the press debate : debating Supreme
Court decisions / Catherine McGlone.— 1st ed.
        p. cm. — (Debating Supreme Court decisions)
    Includes bibliographical references and index.
    ISBN 0-7660-2357-5
    1. Freedom of the press—United States—Juvenile literature. 2. Press law—United
States—Juvenile literature. 3. Libel and slander—United States—Juvenile literature.
4. Sullivan, L. B.—Trials, litigation, etc.—Juvenile literature. 5. New York Times
Company—Trials, litigation, etc.—Juvenile literature. I. Title: New York Times versus
Sullivan and the freedom of the press debate. II. Title. III. Series.
KF4774.M356 2005
342.7308'53—dc22

                                                              2004026781

Printed in the United States of America

10 9 8 7 6 5 4 3 2 1

To Our Readers: We have done our best to make sure that all Internet Addresses in this
book were active and appropriate when we went to press. However, the author and publisher
have no control over and assume no liability for the material available on those Internet sites
or on other Web sites they may link to. Any comments or suggestions can be sent by e-mail
to comments@enslow.com or to the address on the back cover.

Illustration Credits: AP/Wide World, pp. 8, 79; Hemera Image Express, pp. 2,
90; Library of Congress, pp. 17, 47, 61, 69; *The New York Times*, p. 34.

Cover Illustrations: Background, Artville; photographs, Library of Congress.

Contents

chapter 1

The 1960s and the Civil Rights Movement

In the 1960s, Elvis Presley was at the top of the pop music charts and Chubby Checker's dance "the Twist" was a new craze that was sweeping the nation. The Barbie doll was a new toy that amused children from coast to coast. Richard Nixon and John F. Kennedy debated on television as part of the 1960 presidential election. Political tension with Cuba heated to a boiling point.

The 1960s was also a decade of great change and turmoil for the United States. The struggle for civil rights for African Americans was at its peak. Throughout the South, African Americans fought for their place on buses, lunch counters, schools, and voting booths. Often, though, people who challenged the racial system in states in the Deep South, such as

Alabama and Mississippi, were met with physical violence, threats, and arrests. These struggles and challenges were rarely reported in national newspapers. At times, the arrests of local African Americans made the paper. However, the coverage was not widespread. While segregation laws were national, the problem was a southern one.

Rosa Parks and the Montgomery Bus Boycott

Rosa Parks was a seamstress for the Montgomery Fair department store in Montgomery, Alabama. On December 1, 1955, she ended her workweek and boarded a bus to go home. She took her seat in the rear of the bus as was required by Alabama law. When the front section of the bus had filled with passengers, the driver ordered her to give up her seat to a white passenger. There were not separate sections for African-American and white passengers; white passengers were entitled by law to all the seats on the bus. She refused. Rosa Parks was arrested.

Black citizens of Montgomery organized a boycott of the public buses because of Rosa Parks's arrest. One boycott leader was a young clergyman named Martin Luther King, Jr. The organizers urged people to find ways to get to work without using the city buses. They encouraged them to use taxis, form car pools, ride bicycles, or walk. Their protest was a success. Car pools transported about ten thousand people to their jobs each day. Montgomery officials wanted to put an end to the protest so the citizens would use the public buses again. The leaders of the boycotts were charged with crimes and indicted. They would be tried as criminals for their actions.

The officials' plan backfired. The indictments brought national attention to segregation in the South. News broadcasts of the indictments carried the message of segregation to people all over the country. It gave people around the nation the chance to learn about segregation in the South through news reports. The success of the boycott sparked the formation of several civil rights organizations. One of them was the Southern Christian Leadership Conference (SCLC).

Peaceful Protests

College students throughout the South conducted sit-ins. A sit-in is a peaceful demonstration, in an effort to make a statement. People organize and as a group sit together and refuse to move. They hope that their nonviolent unity will bring attention to a particular message or issue. Ella J. Baker, formerly of the SCLC, called an organizational meeting, and on April 17, 1960, started the Student Nonviolent Coordinating Committee. The response was huge. Nearly three hundred young

Rosa Parks poses for her booking photo after being arrested during the Montgomery bus boycott in 1956. Parks's arrest the previous December sparked a city-wide protest that brought worldwide attention to injustices in the American South.

men and women came to this first meeting. It showed that there was a growing interest among African-American students to launch their own desegregation movement.[1] For many, the sit-ins were an opportunity to protest the fact that African Americans were not welcome to sit at the lunch counters at public restaurants and coffee shops. Since blacks were not allowed to enroll in all-white colleges in the South, sit-ins on campuses were designed to show the inequality of education between African Americans and whites.

Silent marches in cities and at town halls became the trademark of these student groups. In 1960, twenty-five hundred people marched silently on the Nashville City Hall. Bernard Lee was president of this student movement at the Alabama State College in Montgomery. Lee led the first sit-in in Montgomery. He organized thirty-five African-American men to sit at the Montgomery County Courthouse snack bar, where they were prohibited. The governor of Alabama responded by having nine of the students expelled from Alabama State College. After the protest, Bernard Lee said, "We have taken up the struggle for freedom without counting the cost. . . . We expect to be thrown in jail . . . but we shall continue to protest and fight for our rights in the court."[2]

"Heed Their Rising Voices"

In 1960, the news of the day rarely featured coverage of the civil rights movement. There were no Internet and no cable television news stations delivering minute-by-minute news from around the world into American homes. On March 29, 1960, *The New York Times* headlines announced that President Eisenhower had met with the British prime minister at Camp David to discuss a proposal with the Soviet Union in a nuclear test ban. In other news, Mrs. Eisenhower was featured for sporting a new hairstyle. Radio City Music Hall presented Doris Day and David Niven in the movie *Please Don't Eat the Daisies*. A recipe in *The New York Times*, in an article featuring economical menus, was for Liver Loaf.

Advertisements in *The New York Times* on March 29, 1960, show what things cost then. An eight-day vacation to Bermuda, including airfare and hotel, cost $215 per person; Abercrombie & Fitch offered its imported silk neckties for $3.50.[3]

In the newspaper that day, one page would have special historical significance: page 25. A group of southern African Americans assembled to raise awareness of the civil rights movement. They also wanted to raise money to support Martin Luther King, Jr. The group was called "the Committee to Defend Martin Luther King and the Struggle for Freedom in the South."

On March 29, 1960, the committee bought a full-page ad in *The New York Times*.

The advertisement was entitled "Heed Their Rising Voices." It outlined ways in which police had abused southern black students. The advertisement stated that after Montgomery students had sung "My Country, 'Tis of Thee" on the steps of the state capitol, "their leaders were expelled from school." It also said that "truckloads of police armed with shotguns and tear-gas ringed the Alabama State College Campus." According to the advertisement, "when the entire student body protested to state authorities by refusing to register, their dining hall was padlocked in an attempt to starve them into submission."[4]

The advertisement charged that southerners had responded to Dr. King's peaceful protest with "intimidation and violence." It stated that Dr. King had been arrested seven times for such minor offenses as loitering and speeding. The arrests, the ad went on, were to disguise "their real purpose . . . to remove him physically as the leader to whom students and millions of others—look for guidance and support, and thereby intimidate *all* leaders who may rise in the South."[5] Sixty-four prominent Americans signed the advertisement, including Eleanor Roosevelt and many noted Hollywood actors. Their signatures showed their support of the committee and the civil rights movement.

Police Commissioner Sullivan Sues

L. B. Sullivan was the elected police commissioner of Montgomery in 1960. Sullivan was not mentioned in the *Times* advertisement, but he thought it was about him. He thought that since he was in charge of the police department, the statements about unscrupulous police activity were a reflection on him. Alabama governor John Patterson also felt the advertisement reflected on himself. Both Sullivan and Governor Patterson demanded that *The New York Times* print a retraction of the statements in the advertisement.

A retraction is a statement that a newspaper publishes to "take back" words that were published. By printing a retraction, a newspaper has an opportunity to decrease its potential damages in a libel action. A retraction is a chance for a newspaper to clarify an inaccuracy in something published. It differs from a correction, where the newspaper corrects specific facts. If a newspaper misspells a person's name or prints the wrong name of the football player who scores the winning touchdown, it may print a correction. When a newspaper does not clarify inaccuracies by printing a retraction, a jury can award punitive damages. Punitive damages are awarded to punish the offender for its conduct.

Commissioner Sullivan wrote a letter to *The New York Times* on April 8, 1960, demanding a retraction. The newspaper's managers were puzzled by Sullivan's complaints that the "Heed Their Rising Voices" ad was about him. They asked Sullivan to help them investigate the conflict by advising them how he thought the ad pertained to him. Sullivan never answered the letter. The *Times* did, however, publish a retraction for Governor Patterson. In May 1960, it published a retraction apologizing for statements about his "grave misconduct."[6]

Sullivan sued *The New York Times* in Alabama state court for defamation. Defamation is legally defined as false statements that harm a person's reputation. Libel and slander are two specific types of defamation. Libel refers to printed statements, and slander refers to oral statements. A defamation lawsuit based on statements in a newspaper would be a case of libel. The all-white Alabama jury awarded Sullivan $500,000.

Roughly 394 copies of the edition of *The New York Times* were sold or distributed in Alabama, 35 in Montgomery County. National circulation for *The New York Times* for that day was approximately 650,000 copies. Today, the *Times* sells 1.1 million copies of the paper daily, and 1.7 million copies on Sundays. Today, the full-page ad would cost $110,565.00.[7]

The lawsuit triggered a four-year legal battle that began on the pages of *The New York Times* and ended in the hallowed halls of the United States Supreme Court. The Committee to Defend Martin Luther King and the Struggle for Freedom in the South had formed to gain national attention to their cause. They never could have imagined that their cause would spark a national debate on the First Amendment and freedom of the press. What followed their cause were a hard-fought debate on the meaning of the First Amendment and a landmark Supreme Court ruling on the freedom of the press.

chapter 2

The Founding Fathers and the First Amendment

In the twenty-first century, it is difficult for Americans to imagine an America without certain things: individual rights, three branches of government, two major political parties, freedom to criticize the government. But if we could travel back in time to Philadelphia 1777, we would find that American life then was much different from life today. In fact, the original United States Constitution did not contain a guarantee of the freedom of the press when it was first written and ratified.

Congress of Confederation

After breaking away from British rule, the thirteen colonies, as a new nation, had to set up a government. The leaders, whom today we call the Founding Fathers, wanted to make sure that the government reflected the reasons they had broken away from Great Britain. In 1779, each of the thirteen colonies sent its leaders to Philadelphia. These delegates gathered to outline the new nation's government. They debated over state boundaries, court systems, taxes, control of the unexplored western territories, and representation in Congress.

The result of this discussion was the Articles of Confederation, ratified in 1781. The articles created a confederation of states and a central government. The new government had a legislature with a single house of Congress. Each state had one vote in the congress. This new Congress did not have the power to collect taxes or regulate trade. The country often spent more money than it earned. The Articles of Confederation did not provide the country with either a president or a court system.

It was not long before it became apparent that the Articles of Confederation did not create unity among the states. The lack of a strong, central government created problems among the states. Individual states had different ideas about commerce, money, and voting. Recognizing the flaws in the Articles of Confederation, James Madison of Virginia and Alexander Hamilton of New York planned a second national meeting. Again, the delegates headed to Philadelphia in 1787.

The Constitution and Individual Rights

Neither the Articles of Confederation nor the original Constitution mentioned what Americans today refer to as their constitutional rights. Freedom of religion, freedom of speech, freedom of association, freedom from unreasonable searches and seizures, and freedom from cruel and unusual punishment were not listed in the original documents.

James Madison was Virginia's delegate to the Philadelphia convention. In Virginia, Madison had worked closely with Thomas Jefferson to guarantee religious freedom for Virginia's citizens. Madison knew these rights were critical to the success of the new nation. He remembered that many people had come to America in the first place because their rights in England had been threatened.

At the first session of Congress in 1789, the representatives wrote the Bill of Rights, the first ten

James Madison was instrumental in adding the Bill of Rights to the U.S. Constitution. He proposed the First Amendment, which guarantees freedom of the press along with other important liberties.

amendments to the Constitution. Madison called these individual freedoms "the great rights of mankind." He proposed the First Amendment on June 8, 1789. His original draft read: "The people shall not be deprived or abridged of their right to speak, to write, or to publish their sentiments; and the freedom of the press, as one of the great bulwarks of liberty, shall be inviolable."[1] Individual state conventions had also addressed the freedom of speech and press. The Pennsylvania state constitution had proposed: "That the people have a right to freedom of speech, of writing, and of publishing their sentiments, therefore, the freedom of the press shall not be restrained by any law of the United States."[2]

In its entirety, the First Amendment reads:

> Congress shall make no law respecting an establishment of religion, or prohibiting the free exercise thereof; or abridging the freedom of speech, or of the press; or the right of the people peaceably to assemble, and to petition the Government for a redress of grievances.

The Sedition Act of 1798

Whatever the founders actually intended by the First Amendment, it is generally agreed that its major purpose was to protect the citizens and to allow them free discussion of the government's operations.[3] It might seem that the First Amendment gave the new Americans the right to speak, write, or publish anything, even criticism of the government. However, that freedom to speak freely about the government has been tested again and again in the two centuries since its birth.

In 1798, Congress passed the Sedition Act. Sedition is speaking, writing, or acting against the government, or trying to overthrow the government in an unlawful way. The Sedition Act made it a crime, punishable by up to two years in jail, to criticize the government. It prohibited anyone to "write, print, utter or publish . . . any false, scandalous and malicious writing . . . against the government of the United States, or either house of the Congress . . . or the President. . . . "[4] In all, fourteen men were charged with violations of the Sedition Act. They included newspaper editors as well as private citizens. In one case, a member of the House of Representatives was charged for writing a letter to the editor of the *Vermont Journal.*

David Brown was an American who tested the Sedition Act. He would walk through Massachusetts' towns, speaking ill of the federal government. He criticized land speculation, treatment of foreigners, the Stamp Act, the Sedition Act, and land tax. He was prosecuted, convicted, sentenced to eighteen months in prison, and fined $450.

When Thomas Jefferson became president in 1801, one of his first acts as president was to pardon all the people who had been convicted of violating the Sedition Act, which was allowed to expire. In a letter to Abigail Adams, Jefferson explained his opposition. He told her he felt as if the Sedition Act was as evil as the government telling the people how to worship.[5] Jefferson, a strong proponent of individual freedoms, believed that the act was fundamentally un-American. Because of its short life, the Sedition Act was never challenged and tested in the Supreme Court. The citizens of the United States were able to give their opinions of the government. They could speak freely about their leaders without fear of being punished. Individual citizens and journalists alike could write about the events and people of their government in the newspapers.

Twentieth-Century Laws that Restricted Speech and Press

After the Sedition Act expired, there was very little activity on the issues of speech and press for over one hundred years. Before World War I, only a small number of cases had raised the issue, but there was a reason for that. The First Amendment reads, "Congress shall make no law . . . abridging the freedom of speech, or of the press." Quite simply, Congress had not passed any such laws. Without such laws, there was no need to challenge the free speech and press clauses of the First Amendment.

When the United States entered World War I in 1917, the mood of the country changed. Patriotism was rampant. War is an emotional national issue.

Some citizens support a war, while others oppose it. Each side feels compelled to voice its opinions on the war. In this atmosphere, Congress passed the Espionage Act of 1917. Espionage is the act of spying—secretly watching the words and actions of another person or a group of people. The Espionage Act made it a crime to refuse duty in the military or to interfere with the recruitment and enlistment of men and women into the armed services. People who spoke out against American involvement with World War I were prosecuted under the Espionage Act. However, they argued that they had the freedom of speech and the press to give their opinions.

During the twentieth century, the constitutionality of certain types of speech were tested. Both spoken words and printed words fall into the category of the First Amendment. The Supreme Court has decided many cases involving different types of speech. Some types have been given the protection of the First Amendment. The government cannot restrict these types of speech and press. These include protesting a war, poking fun at famous people, or burning a flag. The Supreme Court has decided that certain types of speech are not protected by the First Amendment. These include speech that is obscene, encourages people to commit a crime, leads to immediate lawless behavior, interferes with a war, or causes a panic.

Libel: Protected or Unprotected Speech?

Libel is written defamation. Libel occurs when someone writes something false about another person and it causes harm to the person's reputation. It must be more than just an error, such as writing that a person is wearing a blue shirt when he is actually wearing a red shirt. What is written must be important enough to injure the subject's reputation. For a long time, libel was in the category of unprotected speech. Commissioner Sullivan sued *The New York Times* for libel, claiming that the "Heed Their Rising Voices" advertisement maligned his character. The Alabama jury agreed and awarded him $500,000. The *Times* disagreed. They viewed this seemingly ordinary libel case as an all-out assault on the freedom of the press. What followed was a test of the First Amendment and the constitutional privilege of the freedom of the press.

How Can Flag Burning Be Speech?

Flag burning has been classified as speech because it is an activity with a symbolic message. By burning an American flag, a person is expressing his or her disapproval of the United States government. This activity is protected by the First Amendment.

chapter 3

Freedom of the Press: History and Cases

As with all areas of law, the law of the freedom of the press is evolutionary. It grows and changes over time. The freedom of the press begins with the First Amendment, but it does not end there. The meaning of the First Amendment has been tested and challenged by people who claim that the government has restricted their "speech" or "press." If a person or group feels its freedom of speech is being restricted by laws, it goes to court.

However, it was not until World War I that the issue of freedom of speech and press became significantly contested. At that time, laws were enacted that curtailed speech and press, so challenges began over the words and meaning of the First Amendment. Different types of speech and press have been brought to the Supreme Court for a determination of whether or not they enjoy First Amendment protection.

World War I

When the United States entered World War I, patriotism around the country swelled. Pride in America grew. At the same time, Americans became skeptical of foreign governments and enemies. Congress acted in response to this skepticism. In 1917, it passed the Espionage Act.

Shortly after the act was passed, the United States postmaster general enforced it. He refused to allow a revolutionary magazine called *The Masses* to be distributed in the mails. *The Masses* was a propagandist magazine. In August 1917, its publication included articles and cartoons that criticized the United States military draft and its role in World War I.

The publisher of *The Masses* went to court to try to stop the postmaster general from refusing to mail their magazine. The postmaster argued that the magazine violated the Espionage Act.[1] The case was heard in a federal district court in New York. The court ordered the postmaster general to continue to mail the magazine.

Judge Learned Hand, who became one of the country's most distinguished jurists of the early twentieth century, allowed the magazine to be mailed and wrote the opinion for the case. Judge Hand wrote that the right to criticize the government is the privilege of people who live in a free nation where free expression and opinion is the "ultimate source of authority." The case was quickly reversed on appeal, so that the postmaster general won; the magazine was banned from being mailed. The case was not appealed to the United States Supreme Court.[2] Despite this, the case is important because it marks the first modern-day exercise of the freedom of the press.

"Clear and Present Danger"

The Espionage Act reached the Supreme Court in 1919, with three landmark cases: *Schenck* v. *United States*, *Debs* v. *United States*, and *Abrams* v. *United States*. Justice Oliver Wendell Holmes wrote two of the three opinions for the Court. Justice Holmes became a strong voice for the First Amendment in the early part of the twentieth century. His opinions helped shape the freedom of speech and press that Americans currently enjoy.

Charles Schenck was an American socialist who was sending leaflets to men who had been drafted to serve during World War I. The leaflets told people, "Assert Your Rights" and not to participate in the war. It encouraged people to dodge the draft. Justice Holmes acknowledged:

In many places and in ordinary times the defendants (Schenck and his group) in saying all that was said in the circular would have been within their constitutional rights. But the character of every act depends on the circumstances in which it is done. The most stringent protection of free speech would not protect a man in falsely shouting fire in a theatre and causing a panic.[3]

Therefore, the Court ruled that "the question in every case is whether the words are used in such circumstances and are of such a nature as to create a clear and present danger." Since Schenck was getting in the way of military recruitment during a time of war, the leaflets were deemed a "clear and present danger" that would not be protected by the First Amendment. Because of the United States' involvement in the war against Germany, the Schenck leaflets failed the "clear and present danger" test. The convictions were affirmed.

This "clear and present danger" test was extended to the second of the three Espionage Act cases, *Debs* v. *United States*. Eugene V. Debs was convicted under the Espionage Act and served three years in jail for making an antiwar speech. He had printed a document opposing the war, calling "the declaration of war by our Governments a crime against the people of the United States." He encouraged opposition to the war. At his trial, Debs had told the jury, "I have been accused of obstructing the war. I admit it. Gentlemen, I abhor war. I would oppose the war if I stood alone."[4] The Court upheld Debs's conviction.

The third case in the trilogy of Espionage Act cases was *Abrams* v. *United States*.[5] Jacob Abrams and his cohorts had rented a room in a New York City building, installed printing machines, and printed leaflets. The papers denounced President Woodrow Wilson and the United States' participation in World War I. Some of the messages were printed in the Yiddish language. The group threw the leaflets from the windows of the building, showering their messages onto the city streets.

The Supreme Court upheld the *Abrams* conviction, but this time, Justice Holmes wrote a dissenting opinion. In the dissent, the justice gives his reasons why the court should have decided the case the other way. Justice Holmes dissented in *Abrams* because he thought the papers did not present a "clear and imminent danger" as they had in *Schenck* and *Debs*. Justice Holmes's dissent in *Abrams* is important because it demonstrates his conviction of the significance of the freedom of speech and press. He wrote,

> Congress certainly cannot forbid all effort to change the mind of the country. . . . I believe the defendants had as much right to publish [the leaflets] as the Government has to publish the Constitution of the United States.[6]

While each of these cases limited the freedom of the press, they were important because they opened the discussion about the freedom of the press and speech. They established the foundation for cases that would be heard in years to come.

Prior Restraint and Censorship

One of the major concepts associated with the freedom of the press is that the government cannot stop speech before it is spoken. Doing so is known as prior restraint. The prohibition against prior restraint means that a person or publisher cannot be stopped from speaking or printing freely— although they may be punished if the words violate the law. American's abhorrence of prior restraints dates back to the Founding Fathers. They drafted the Bill of Rights following a period in England when nothing could be printed without first being cleared by the government.[7]

In 1925, Minnesota had a law that allowed the government to stop or curtail "malicious, scandalous and defamatory" newspapers or periodicals.[8] J. M. Near published a newspaper, *The Saturday Press*, that printed stories about Minneapolis gangsters, gambling, bootlegging, and racketeering. The articles accused local police of ignoring the conduct. In the state court, Near was enjoined (stopped) from printing the newspaper, because it violated the law. The Minnesota Supreme Court ruled that the statute did not violate the Constitution.[9] When Near appealed his case to the U.S. Supreme Court, he argued that the state's action was a prior restraint that violated the freedom of the press guaranteed in the First Amendment. The Supreme Court reversed the Minnesota court decision. Chief Justice Charles Evans Hughes wrote in the Court's opinion that preventing the publication was a violation of the freedom of the press, and so the Minnesota law was unconstitutional.

Libel

The United States Supreme Court had spoken on the issues of speech that promoted committing a crime or standing in the way of a country at war. It had addressed the prior restraints of speech. In the mid-twentieth century, the Court tackled the content of speech and whether it could punish the speaker for the words that were either spoken or written. In 1942, the Court concluded that offensive types of speech would not be protected by the First Amendment. It included libel as one type of offensive speech. In *Chaplinsky* v. *New Hampshire*, Justice Frank Murphy wrote that preventing and punishing certain types of speech have never presented a constitutional violation:

> These include the lewd and obscene, the profane, the libelous and the insulting or 'fighting' words—those

which by their very utterance inflict injury or tend to incite an immediate breach of the peace.

He concluded that these types of speech had such little social value that they were "outweighed by the social interest in order and morality.[10]

A further examination of libel law came in 1952, in the case of _Beauharnais_ v. _Illinois_.[11] Joseph Beauharnais was convicted under an Illinois law that made it a crime to publish anything that showed "depravity, criminality, unchastity or lack of virtue of a class of citizens of any race, color, creed or religion."[12] Beauharnais had distributed anti-Negro pamphlets on the streets of Chicago. The pamphlet was a petition that would be presented to the mayor of Chicago and the city council. It asked the city to "halt the further encroachment, harassment and invasion of white people, their property, neighborhoods and persons, by the Negro."[13] In a 5–4 decision, the Supreme Court upheld the conviction. Justice Felix Frankfurter wrote the majority opinion in which he analyzed the history of the law of libel in the United States. He noted that every state had a libel law on its books. He relied on the precedent of libel law to support the Court's decision to punish Beauharnais for the pamphlet.

Four justices dissented in the _Beauharnais_ case. In a separate, dissenting opinion, Justice Hugo Black wrote that in a free nation, the legislature had no power or duty to decide what issues its citizens could discuss. He warned that state laws that restrained free expression would threaten self-government. "I reject the holding that either state or nation can punish people for having their say in matters of public concern."[14]

What Could *The New York Times* and Sullivan Expect?

Eight years after the *Beauharnais* decision, Commissioner Sullivan brought his lawsuit against *The New York Times* for libel. In *Beauharnais*, the conviction had been affirmed by one vote. Four of the nine justices disagreed with the result. In 1964, when *The New York Times* went to the Supreme Court, only two members of the Court that had decided *Beauharnais*, Justices Hugo Black and William O. Douglas, were left on the Supreme Court. Both Black and Douglas had dissented in *Beauharnais*. Would their disagreement with their former colleagues mean that they wanted libel to have the protection of the First Amendment? Did the disagreement signal a new page in the history books for First Amendment law?

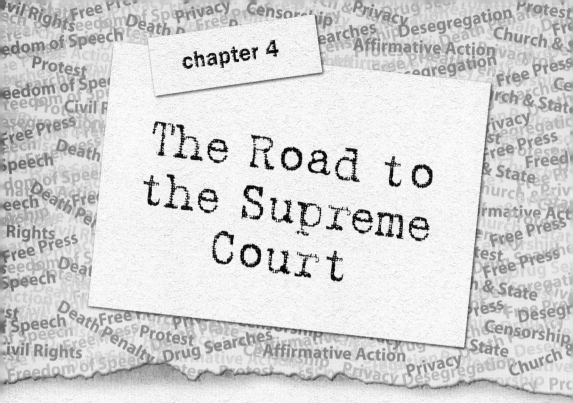

chapter 4

The Road to the Supreme Court

Oyez, oyez, oyez! All persons having business before the Honorable, the Supreme Court of the United States, are admonished to draw near and give their attention, for the Court is now sitting. God save the United States and this Honorable Court.

A lawsuit's road to the United States Supreme Court is a long one, with many steps along the way. A case is first heard in a state court or a federal district court. When the case is decided by judge or jury, one side wins, and the other loses. The party that loses the case may wish to appeal the decision. That is, they may ask for another, higher court to review the decision of the lower court. The

United States Supreme Court is the nation's highest such appeals court.

Commissioner Sullivan Sues *The New York Times*

When *The New York Times* did not print a retraction, Commissioner Sullivan filed a lawsuit in Montgomery County in Alabama state court. He claimed that the "Heed Their Rising Voices" advertisement libeled him. The trial took place November 1–3, 1960; Judge Walter Burgwyn Jones presided. T. Eric Embry was the lawyer who defended the *Times*. M. Roland Nachman, Jr., was the lawyer who presented Commissioner Sullivan's case to the jury.

There were thirty-six men from whom the lawyers would pick their jury. Of the potential jurors, only two were African Americans, and both were stricken from the jury pool. A jury of twelve white men was selected. Nachman told the jury that Sullivan should win the case so that *The New York Times* would not libel other officials in the future. He also said he hoped that other newspapers would be deterred from printing libelous falsehoods. Embry argued that the advertisement could not be libel because it did not mention Sullivan at all.[1]

Components of a Libel Action

To win a case of libel, a plaintiff has to convince a jury of three elements. First, he must show that

This advertisement appeared in The New York Times *on March 29, 1960. It would lead to a Supreme Court case on the freedom of the press.*

The Advertisement

"The growing movement of peaceful mass demon-strations by Negroes is something new in the South. . . . Let Congress heed their rising voices, for they will be heard."

—*New York Times* editorial
Saturday, March 19, 1960

Heed Their Rising Voices

As the whole world knows by now, thousands of Southern Negro students are engaged in widespread non-violent demonstrations in positive affirmation of the right to live in human dignity as guaranteed by the U.S. Constitution and the Bill of Rights. In their efforts to uphold these guarantees, they are being met by an unprecedented wave of terror by those who would deny and negate that document which the whole world looks upon as setting the pattern for modern freedom. . . .

In Orangeburg, South Carolina, when 400 students peacefully sought to buy doughnuts and coffee at lunch counters in the business district, they were forcibly ejected, tear-gassed, soaked to the skin in freezing weather with fire hoses, arrested en masse and herded into an open barbed-wire stockade to stand for hours in the bitter cold.

In Montgomery, Alabama, after students sang "My Country, 'Tis of Thee" on the State Capitol steps, their leaders were expelled from school, and truckloads of police armed with shotguns and tear-gas ringed the Alabama State College Campus.

When the entire student body protested to state authorities by refusing to re-register, their dining hall was padlocked in an attempted to starve them into submission.

In Tallahassee, Atlanta, Nashville, Savannah, Greensboro, Memphis, Richmond, Charlotte, and a host of other cities in the South, young American teenagers, in face of the entire weight of official state apparatus and police power, have boldly stepped forth as protagonists of democracy. Their courage and amazing restraint have inspired millions and given a new dignity to the cause of freedom.

Small wonder that the Southern violators of the Constitution fear this new, non-violent brand of freedom fighter . . . even as they fear the upswelling right-to-vote movement. Small wonder that they are determined to destroy the one man who, more than any other, symbolizes the new spirit now sweeping the South—the Rev. Dr. Martin Luther King, Jr., world-famous leader of the Montgomery Bus Protest. For it is his doctrine of non-violence which has inspired and guided the students in their widening wave of sit-ins; and it [is] this same Dr. King who founded and is president of the Southern Christian Leadership Conference—the organization which is spearheading the surging right-to-vote movement. Under Dr. King's direction the Leadership Conference conducts Student Workshops and Seminars in the philosophy and technique of non-violent resistance.

Again and again the Southern violators have answered Dr. King's peaceful protests with intimidation and violence. They have bombed his home almost killing his wife and child. They have assaulted his person. They have arrested him seven times—for "speeding," "loitering" and similar "offenses." And now they have charged him with "perjury"—a felony under which they could imprison him for ten years. Obviously, their real purpose is to remove him physically as the leader to whom the students and millions of others—look for guidance and support, and thereby to intimidate all leaders who may rise in the South. Their strategy is to behead this affirmative movement, and thus to demoralize Negro Americans and weaken their will to struggle. The defense of Martin Luther King, spiritual leader of the student sit-in movement, clearly, therefore, is an integral part of the total struggle for freedom in the South.

Decent-minded Americans cannot help but applaud the creative daring of the students and the quiet heroism of Dr. King. But this is one of those moments in the stormy history of Freedom when men and women of good will must do more than applaud the rising-to-glory of others. The America whose good name hangs in the balance before a watchful world, the America whose heritage of Liberty these Southern Upholders of the Constitution are defending, is our America as well as theirs. . .

We must heed their rising voices—yes—but we must add our own.

We must extend ourselves above and beyond moral support and render the material help so urgently needed by those who are taking the risks, facing jail, and even death in a glorious re-affirmation of our Constitution and its Bill of Rights.

⟶

We urge you to join hands with our fellow Americans in the South by supporting, with your dollars, this Combined Appeal for all three needs— the defense of Martin Luther King—the support of the embattled students—and the struggle for the right to vote.[2]

⟵

the defendant made a publication. Second, the publication has to contain a defamatory statement. The statement must be false, in a significant way, and not merely incorrect. For instance, if a newspaper reports that a baseball player hit a fly ball to center field when he actually hit it to left field, the hitter cannot claim that he was libeled. Third, the defamatory statement has to be about the plaintiff.

When Sullivan sued *The New York Times*, his lawyers concentrated on the third and sixth paragraphs of the advertisement, which mentioned police conduct. The third paragraph of the ad said that armed police had ringed the college campus. The sixth paragraph said that the police had arrested Martin Luther King, Jr., seven times.[3]

Several of the statements in the ad were not accurate:

1. The advertisement stated that students had sung "My Country, 'Tis of Thee" on the steps of

the state capitol; in reality, the song had been "The Star-Spangled Banner."

2. Students were not expelled for demonstrating at the capitol, but for conducting a sit-in at a courthouse cafeteria.

3. The police had not "ringed the Alabama State College Campus," but had massed on one side.

4. The student dining hall had not been padlocked after students refused to re-register.

5. Martin Luther King had been arrested four times, not seven times.

An equally important aspect of the case was whether or not the defamatory statements were "of and concerning" the plaintiff. Commissioner Sullivan testified at the trial that he thought the statements referred to him. "I certainly do. The statements are concerning arrests of people and truckloads of police. I feel they are associated with me."[4]

The New York Times called several witnesses. Gershon Aronson described the process through which the committee had placed the ad. Another witness, Vincent Redding, was the manager of the *Times* advertising acceptability department. He testified that he approved the ad because it had many signatures of well-known and well-respected citizens.[5]

After the parties were through presenting evidence and calling witnesses, the judge instructed the jury on the law. In this situation, the judge read a list of issues that the jury must decide, and he explained to them the law relating to the issues. Judge Jones told the twelve men that their only job was to decide three things: (1) whether *The New York Times* had published the ad, (2) whether the ad was about Commissioner Sullivan, and (3) what, if any, the damages should be. Damages in a lawsuit are the amount of money, if any, that a plaintiff is awarded because of the conduct of the defendant.

Judge Jones told the jury that the statements in the ad were libelous *per se*. (*Per se* means "in itself.") That meant that the words alone were defamatory and harmed the reputation of Commissioner Sullivan. Judge Jones instructed the jury that under Alabama law, a person is presumed to be damaged by defamatory statements—in other words, if they decided *The New York Times* had published the advertisement and that it was about Commissioner Sullivan, then they had to determine an amount of money to award Commissioner Sullivan.

The jury considered the case for two hours and twenty minutes. They awarded Commissioner Sullivan $500,000. The Alabama Supreme Court agreed with the jury and upheld the decision on August 30, 1962. The verdict and $500,000 award stood.

Appeal to the United States Supreme Court

One of the United States Supreme Court's primary functions is judicial review—that is, to determine the constitutionality of laws. However, the Constitution does not contain a provision actually granting the Court the power to decide whether laws are constitutional. In 1803, the Supreme Court defined its role in the case of *Marbury* v. *Madison*. The case concluded that the Constitution, with the Bill of Rights, was designed to have three branches of government working within a system of checks and balances. That is, each branch acts as a check, or limiting force, on the others, to balance power between the branches. The authors of the Bill of Rights had intended the three branches of government—the president, the Congress, and the courts—to work together, with no one branch having more power than the others. Therefore, the Court needed the power to strike down a law enacted by Congress if the law conflicted with the Constitution. In *Marbury* v. *Madison*, the Supreme Court assumed its responsibility and authority to review acts of Congress and strike down those that conflicted with the Constitution.[6]

How Does a Case Get to the Court?

Federal law gives the United States Supreme Court jurisdiction to hear certain cases.[7] (Jurisdiction means the power and authority of a court to hear and to decide a case.[8]) Cases reach the Supreme Court by either of two means. First, certain cases, such as death penalty convictions, can be appealed "as of right," meaning that these cases will be heard directly by the Supreme Court. The majority of cases, though, must be taken by a writ of _certiorari_ (ser-she-o-RAR-ee). A party who wants to bring a case to the Supreme Court must make a preliminary application to the Court, asking for the case to be heard. The Court grants certiorari "only for compelling reasons."[9]

In 1949, Chief Justice Fred Vinson described the role of the Supreme Court and the exercise of certiorari:

> The function of the Supreme Court is, therefore, to resolve conflicts of opinion on federal questions that have arisen among lower courts, to pass upon questions of wide import under the Constitution, laws and treaties of the United States, and to exercise supervisory power over lower federal courts. If we took every case in which an interesting legal question is raised, . . . we would not fulfill the Constitutional and statutory responsibilities placed upon the Court. Those of you whose petitions for certiorari are granted by the Supreme Court will know, therefore, that you are, in a sense, prosecuting or defending class actions; that you represent not only your clients, but tremendously important principles, upon which are based the plans, hopes and aspirations of a great many people throughout the country.[10]

The Petition of *The New York Times* for Certiorari

After losing in the Alabama Supreme Court, the attorneys for *The New York Times* had ninety days to present an application for certiorari to the United States Supreme Court.[11] The party applying to the Supreme Court is called the "petitioner." Their petition for certiorari has to contain a short, concise question or questions that they want the Supreme Court to answer. Their questions have to show that the case violates the Constitution or raises an important issue of federal law. The *Times* asked the Court whether the Alabama Supreme Court's ruling about liability violated the First Amendment. Following Justice Vinson's explanation, their question was presented on behalf of all publishers and their ability to print such criticisms. A ruling in favor of *The New York Times* would be a victory for all publishers and the exercise of the First Amendment.

The New York Times hired a constitutional scholar to help them prepare the case for the Supreme Court. Herbert Wechsler was a professor at Columbia Law School. He had appeared before the United States Supreme Court about a dozen times. *The New York Times* had ninety days from the date of the Alabama Supreme Court decision to file the petition for certiorari. Wechsler and his

---

How Many Cases Does the Court Hear?

The Supreme Court receives approximately seven thousand petitions each year. One hundred cases get full review by the court. Another fifty to sixty cases are decided without a full hearing. The Court's written opinions are published in books, and average about five thousand pages per year.[12]

Prior to 1925, the Supreme Court was overburdened with cases. About two hundred fifty cases were filed each court year. In each case, the justices had to read lawyers' briefs, hear oral arguments, and write a decision on the case. Sometimes, it would take up to two years for a party to have its case heard. Then, Congress passed the Judiciary Act of 1925, which gave the Court flexibility over its workload. The act gave the Court the power to decide which cases it would hear.[13] By controlling the cases it hears, the Court can focus on issues of national and constitutional significance and not just oversee decisions of lower federal and state courts.

---

assistant, Marvin Frankel, filed the *Times* petition for certiorari on November 21, 1962.[14] The *Times* argued that Sullivan should not have won the trial. They said that the law that allowed Sullivan to win damages was the same as laws against seditious libel. The Sedition Act had been allowed to expire because the early Americans realized how severely the law had restricted free speech and press.

Commissioner Sullivan Opposes the Petition

Once *The New York Times* filed its petition for certiorari, Commissioner Sullivan had thirty days to file papers to oppose the newspaper.[15] Sullivan's job as the "respondent" was to convince the Supreme Court not to hear the case. He had to point out to the Court errors of the facts or application of law as set forth in the *Times* petition.

M. Roland Nachman, Jr., one of Sullivan's attorneys at the trial, prepared the brief in opposition. The Sullivan brief was filed on December 15, 1962. It argued that the *Times* had chosen excitement over truth. "*The New York Times*, perhaps the nation's most influential newspaper, stooped to circulate a paid advertisement . . . which libeled [Sullivan] with violent, inflammatory and devastating language."[16]

The Supreme Court Takes the Case

The Supreme Court then issued its ruling on whether it would hear the case.[17] On January 7, 1962, the Supreme Court granted a writ of certiorari to *The New York Times*.

Now that the Supreme Court had agreed to hear the case of *New York Times* v. *Sullivan*, the parties had to first present written briefs. A brief is a small book that tells the story of the case. It includes a summary of the facts of the case, the applicable law, and an argument on how the parties believe the law applies to the facts.

Since the cases heard by the United States Supreme Court are representative of bigger issues that have national and constitutional significance, other parties are allowed to file briefs. With the permission of the petitioner and respondent, other interested parties can file *amicus curiae* (friend of the court) briefs. *Amicus* briefs are written by people or groups who share the opinion of one of the parties in the case. The *amicus* party wants the Supreme Court to decide the case a certain way. The *Washington Post* newspaper recognized the important first amendment issue raised by *The New York Times*. Since it was important for the *Post* that *The New York Times* win, it filed an *amicus* brief. Additionally, the American Civil Liberties Union and the New York Civil Liberties Union also filed *amicus* briefs.

After the briefs are filed, the Court schedules the case for oral argument. At oral argument, the lawyer for each petitioner and respondent has thirty minutes to state his case. During that time, the nine justices are seated across the front of the courtroom, in order of seniority, with the Chief Justice at the center. The justices ask questions of the lawyers.

In the days and weeks after oral argument, the justices discuss the case to decide how the court

Martin Luther King, Jr., shown here behind bars in St. Augustine, Florida, was jailed many times for civil disobedience of unjust segregation laws.

47

will rule. Eventually, they vote and render a decision. A party needs only a majority of the votes in order to win. When the Supreme Court rules, one justice serves as the author of the majority opinion. Sometimes, individual justices want to write their own opinion of the case. If they agree with the decision of the court, they write a concurring opinion. If they disagree, they write a dissent.

chapter 5

The Case for The New York Times

After the United States Supreme Court agreed to hear the *New York Times* case, Wechsler and the team of lawyers for the newspaper rolled up their sleeves to work on the case they would present to the Court. They would prepare both a written brief and an oral argument. Louis Loeb and T. Eric Embry, who represented the *Times* at the trial in Alabama, worked with Wechsler. Wechsler's wife, Doris; Marvin Frankel; and another attorney named Ronald Diana completed the team.

The group knew that their case was a difficult challenge. There were two compelling reasons that the Court would be reluctant to reverse the decision of the Alabama Supreme Court. First, appellate courts such as the Supreme Court are very cautious about reversing a jury's verdict. Appellate courts give weight to the fact that the jurors sat through the original trial and heard the live testimony of the witnesses. The jurors made their decisions based on the sights and sounds of the trial. Having sat through the proceeding, they are in the best position to assess how credible the witnesses are.

Secondly, the case of *The New York Times* was difficult because the current law of libel clearly favored Sullivan. Libel was not a type of speech that was protected by the First Amendment. In constitutional law terms, it had always been treated as "outside the scope" of the First Amendment. Libel had never been deemed worthy of First Amendment protection. Courts had held that since libel causes harm to a person's reputation, it was not constitutionally protected. This was the precedent of the law of libel. (A precedent is a prior court decision on an issue used as an example for deciding cases that follow.) Courts try to decide cases based on the principles of earlier cases. Wechsler and his team would have to convince the Supreme Court to overturn this precedent. They would have to find a way to give constitutional protection to false statements and criticism of public officials. They hoped to show that an ordinary state libel action was actually a massive assault on the freedom of the press.

Wechsler decided to present the case for *The New York Times* to the Supreme Court through the story of the Sedition Act. He would tell the history of the act and point out the reasons that it was short-lived. He hoped to convince the justices that the Sedition Act had died an early death because early Americans thrived on debate. American resistance to and rejection of the Sedition Act showed that free speech has always included the right to criticize the government. Now, nearly two hundred years later, he would demonstrate that Alabama's libel law was a violation of this right.

The Brief for *The New York Times*

The *Times* filed its brief with the United States Supreme Court on September 6, 1963. It consisted of ninety printed pages. The brief began with a summary of their argument, which gave the Court a short explanation of the case and the reasons the lower court should be reversed. It discussed the First Amendment protection that should be given to libel. It addressed the question of whether the $500,000 jury verdict violated *The New York Times*'s freedom of the press. It questioned whether there had been sufficient evidence in the trial to justify the jury's finding that the advertisement was defamatory.[1] The brief offered several major points:

Alabama should have applied the First Amendment to the advertisement. The first argument of *The New York Times* was that the Alabama court was wrong to decide that the First Amendment did not protect libelous speech and publications. Alabama had made a mistake in failing to apply the First Amendment to the statements contained in the "Heed Their Rising Voices" advertisement. Wechsler argued that the freedom of speech and the press is a basic constitutional right. The First Amendment was written so that Americans could exchange ideas and opinions freely, especially if they wanted to bring about political and social changes.[2]

The *Times* pointed out several ways in which the Alabama court's holding violated the First Amendment. First, speech should not be suppressed just because it might hurt the reputations of public officers who are the subject of the speech.[3] If that were the case, Wechsler argued, then no one could say anything about a public official except to praise him. Anything else would risk being libelous. Newspapers and other publications, knowing that the publication could be prosecuted for libel, would probably decide not to print such statements, because they would not want to pay the damages. For instance, *The New York Times*, knowing that it might have to pay $500,000 to a police chief for comments published about him, might not run a story or advertisement with language about him. This concept of prior restraint of speech has always been a clear violation of the First Amendment, Wechsler pointed out. It violates the First Amendment because it tends to have a chilling effect, as if it freezes the thoughts and words of Americans.

The lessons of the Sedition Act of 1798. Wechsler next argued that the "Heed their Rising Voices" ad was a political document, in the same way as the pamphlets of those punished under the Sedition Act. The advertisement objected to and protested against alleged police misconduct. Most significantly, it was trying to spark debate about one of the major issues of its time, the civil rights movement.

He pointed out that one lesson of the Sedition Act was that the possibility of harming an official's reputation by false statements did not justify stifling criticism of the official. He recalled that the First Amendment was written at a time when there was strong opposition to the Sedition Act. By enacting the freedom of the press in the First Amendment, it ensured the public's right to criticize the government.

Wechsler noted that the Alabama libel statute was in some ways worse than the Sedition Act. Since the Sedition Act imposed criminal penalties, the plaintiff had to prove the crime. Under

Legal Terms

amicus curiae—Latin for "friend of the court." Organizations that have an interest in a case, but are not directly involved, file *amicus curiae* briefs, stating their opinions, in an attempt to influence the court's final ruling.

appellant or petitioner—In an appeals case, the party that asks the court to reverse the lower court decision.

appellee or respondent—In an appeals case, the party that won the lower court case and asks that the decision stand as is.

brief—A written document submitted to a court to explain the facts of a case and the applicable law. A brief is generally written by one of the parties to persuade the court to rule in its favor.

defense lawyer—The lawyer responsible for defending the accused in a lawsuit or a criminal case.

majority opinion—The ruling and reasoning supported by a majority of appellate court judges in a case. **Concurring opinions** are written by judges who agree with the majority opinion but have different reasons for their views. **Dissenting opinions** are written by judges who disagree with the majority.

oral argument—An opportunity for the parties in a legal action to discuss their case with the court. Lawyers answer questions from the court and explain why their side should win.

precedent—A decision of a court that is considered to be an example of how courts will rule in future cases with the same legal issue.

prosecution lawyer—The lawyer responsible for presenting the case against an accused individual.

writ of certiorari—An order granted by the United States Supreme Court when a party applies to the Court to review the decision of a lower court and the Supreme Court agrees to do so.

the Alabama statute, the damages to the plaintiff's reputation were presumed and did not require proof that the plaintiff's reputation was harmed by the publication.[4]

Protection for political speech. The *Times* next argued that speech of a political nature, even if false, deserved to be protected by the First Amendment. For this proposition, he relied on a 1940 Supreme Court case called *Cantwell* v. *Connecticut*.[5] The *Cantwell* case involved a Jehovah's Witness preacher who traveled through a neighborhood and spoke ill of the Catholic Church. He was convicted of breach of the peace. (Breach of the peace is a violation or disturbance of public tranquility and order.[6])

In reversing the conviction, the Supreme Court observed that religious speech and political speech bore similarities because they both contain the speaker's beliefs. In both politics and religion, what is attractive or believable to one person may be abhorrent to the next. The Court said that to exercise the right to persuade people of our views requires being able to resort "to exaggeration, to vilification of men who have been or are prominent in church or state, and even to false statement."[7]

According to Wechsler, the better way—the American way—to arrive at an "enlightened opinion" is to allow free and open debate. Americans accept the risk of errors along the way, for the greater good of being able to discuss and to debate differences. Therefore, truth cannot be the only test. Speech that is true cannot libel someone. Speech that is false may libel someone, but not in every instance.

Equal immunity. With limited exceptions, anything said by a public official in his or her official capacity cannot be the basis for a libel lawsuit. This is called immunity, and it is a long-standing legal principle. The reason for giving an official this immunity is that the threat of a defamation lawsuit might prevent the official from doing his job vigorously.[8] The immunity applies to the public official no matter whether his statement is true or false. *The New York Times* asserted that citizens and newspapers should have the same immunity when they speak or write about public officials. They should not have to fear potential libel suits, just as public officials do not have to fear them.

Offering an alternative. The *Times* feared that the Court would be reluctant to make a drastic change in the law of libel and give it the protection of the First Amendment. Its lawyers knew that an official's reputation was important. The Court might not agree with *The New York Times*'s argument that the criticism of an official's reputation should be protected by the First Amendment. Wechsler and his team decided to offer some compromise approaches that the Court could take. They offered several ways to prevent huge libel judgments against newspapers, such as Sullivan had won, while protecting the public official's reputation:

⬦ ***Special damages***. The first compromise solution that the *Times* presented was to call for special damages in libel actions by public officials.[9] Under this scenario, a public official could sue a publication for libel but would have to prove that he had sustained a financial loss. (This was in contrast to the law in Alabama at the time of the Sullivan trial that said that damage was presumed if a libelous statement was made—that is, as long as the public official proved that the libelous statement about him was published, he was presumed to have been damaged by it.) Under the proposed special-damages theory, the public official would have to prove his financial loss. If the official had lost his job because of the false statement in the press, he could sue the newspaper and his special damages would be his lost salary. Sullivan could not sue the paper if his reputation had been harmed by a truthful statement.

At the oral argument, Justice John Marshall Harlan asked Sullivan's attorney, M. Roland Nachman, Jr., whether there had been an effort to prove special damages. Nachman responded that one of the *Times*'s trial witnesses had testified that Commissioner Sullivan's reputation had been damaged and that he might not be rehired. However, Nachman admitted that Sullivan had lost no money because of the advertisement.[10]

◇ ***Actual malice***. The second compromise presented to the Court was to allow the official to recover damages only if he proved that the libelous statement was made with actual malice. Malice is intentionally doing a wrongful act without any justification or excuse, so as to cause harm.[11] This standard would require the official to prove that the newspaper knew the printed information was false, yet published it anyway.[12] The official would have a difficult time proving not only that the statement was false, but also that the writer and newspaper knew that the information was false at the time it was published.

Wechsler proposed several reasons that the actual malice standard should apply to these cases. The press is a check on the government. It encourages free debate among citizens and politicians alike. Public officials, by virtue of their position, have a great ability to respond to false statements. They usually have the money or the status to respond if they choose. By choosing to hold public office, they willingly take on the risk of public scrutiny.

◇ ***Was the advertisement about Sullivan?*** Another argument presented by *The New York Times* was that the advertisement was not about Commissioner Sullivan. In the language of the law of libel, the advertisement was not "of and concerning" him. The advertisement did not mention Sullivan by name. Wechsler pointed out that the *Times* could not understand how Sullivan could claim he was libeled.[13] Sullivan had not lost his job or been reprimanded after the publication of the advertisement. There was no indication that his reputation had been hurt because of what was printed in *The New York Times*. Wechsler argued that the Court would have to stretch the facts to find that the advertisement was "of and concerning" Sullivan. After all, his name was not even mentioned in print. During the oral argument before the Supreme Court on March 1, 1964, Wechsler said, "We are at a loss to know precisely in what respect Sullivan was libeled."[14]

◇ ***"There never is a time."*** Finally, *The New York Times* made a compelling statement about the importance of the freedom of the press. It stressed that the freedom of the press is all the more important at times in American history when a major issue or crisis unfolds. The civil rights movement and the critical national struggle for equality among African Americans was under way. This important movement deserved the full exercise of the freedom of the press. According to Wechsler:

> This is not the time—there never is a time—when it would serve the values enshrined in the Constitution to force the

press to curtail its attention to the tensest issues that confront the country or to forego the dissemination of its publications in the areas where the tension is extreme.[15]

◇ ***Amicus arguments***. Both the *Washington Post* and the *Chicago Tribune* filed friend of the court briefs. These two major newspapers certainly had an interest in the outcome of the *New York Times* v. *Sullivan* case. The *Chicago Tribune* pointed out that some modern politicians had tried to silence newspapers as they printed statements about the officials. The *Washington Post*'s brief focused on one of the alternatives that *The New York Times* had offered in its brief. They argued that the First Amendment should protect the press where statements are made and honestly believed to be true.

Oral Argument

In the brief for *The New York Times*, Wechsler made his case based on history, precedent, and common law. Unlike laws that are written by a legislature, common law is the body of law that comes from common use or old customs and which have been later recognized by courts. It has its origin in old English law. His strategy before the nine justices of the Supreme Court at oral argument was to focus on the details of the advertisement. He wanted to demonstrate that the commissioner had suffered no consequences as a result of the publication. He wanted to show

Civil rights marchers in Washington, D.C., in 1963. Herbert Wechsler, one of the attorneys for The New York Times, *called civil rights one of the "tensest issues that confront the country."*

that the advertisement could not be deemed to be about the commissioner. "The case begins with the publication, and ends there as well," he told the Court.[16] He told the Court that the text of the advertisement was a statement of protest, interwoven with a list of events that had occurred in the South. Its goal was to raise both awareness of the movement and money to support the cause. He pointed out that the only person named in the advertisement was Martin Luther King, Jr.

chapter 6

The Case for Commissioner Sullivan

When the United States Supreme Court agreed to hear *The New York Times*'s case, the great burden was on the newspaper. The original trial jury had determined that the *Times* printed the libelous statement about Commissioner Sullivan. The *Times* had to convince the Court to change First Amendment law, which clearly favored Sullivan. The Sullivan case had, until it reached the Supreme Court, gone according to the letter of the law. There were libelous statements allegedly about the plaintiff, and the jury awarded the presumed damages. The jury verdict was entirely in keeping with the Alabama law. Sullivan's job in the Supreme Court case was to convince the justices that nothing special was happening with the *New York Times* case that would warrant reversing the jury's decision. It certainly did not justify a drastic change in the law of libel.

The Sullivan case had several strengths as they approached the Supreme Court. Libel had never been protected by the First Amendment. It was among the types of speech that did not fall under the umbrella of constitutionally protected speech. Libel was seen to diminish the personal reputation of the public official and the credibility of government. Precedent on this issue was solid, and there was no reason to believe the Court would upset it. A change in the law might lead to mistakes, sloppy reporting, and laziness by newspapers and reporters, according to Sullivan's argument. Sullivan noted that reporters might be lax if they had nearly absolute immunity from being sued for libel. Finally, changing the law could discourage public service, because without such protection, people might not run for public office and expose themselves to criticism by newspapers.

Brief for the Respondent

Despite his position as the favorite in the contest, Commissioner Sullivan had to present a solid, written argument to the Supreme Court. The Sullivan brief was written by M. Roland Nachman, Jr., with the assistance of Robert E. Steiner III, Sam Rice Baker, and Calvin Whitesell. The sixty-six-page brief began by pointing out that *The New York Times*'s advertisement had met its goals. The paper wanted to portray criminal police activity, and in the words of the advertisement, an "unprecedented wave of terror" that followed from the students singing "My Country, 'Tis of Thee" on the steps of the state capitol building. The Sullivan team stated that the advertisement had falsely stated that innocent people were expelled from their schools. The ad charged that the police engaged in the "ringing of a college campus with truckloads of police armed with shotguns and tear-gas [and] padlocking of the dining hall to starve protesting students into submission."[1]

Sullivan's team pointed out that whenever challenged, the Supreme Court did not extend First Amendment protection to libel. "This Court has repeatedly held that libelous utterances are not protected by the Constitution," Nachman wrote in the brief.[2] He cited many cases the Supreme Court had already decided that supported this proposition. He wrote that in the ten years before *New York Times* v. *Sullivan*, the Supreme Court had denied review of forty-four libel cases. Nachman also pointed out that advertisements are different from news stories or editorial columns. This is because someone, like the Committee to Defend Martin Luther King and the Struggle for Freedom in the South, paid for the advertisement. *The New*

York Times was sued rather than the committee because the *Times* published the advertisement. In newspaper language, it is known as an "editorial advertisement." It did not matter that *The New York Times* was paid to print the advertisement. The goal was to encourage and to enable people who are not part of the media to exercise their freedom of speech and press. Advertising is a way an ordinary citizen gains access to publishing.[3]

Libel *Per Se*

Once Nachman had given the precedent for his position that libel earned no protection from the U.S. Constitution, he moved on to the specifics of the ad. The advertisement, he argued, was libel *per se* under the law. Libel per se means that on its own, without any other evidence or inferences, the publication is libelous. Alabama law defined libel as a false publication that damages a person, defames his reputation, brings him into public contempt, or charges him with a crime.[4] Alabama's law was similar to laws in most other states in 1960. Nachman opposed the *Times*'s position that the content of the advertisement was merely political criticism. He stated in the brief that *The New York Times* was asking the court for a special favor: to protect newspapers such as themselves from huge libel judgments, thus allowing them the freedom to print false statements about public officials.

Nachman gave examples of what could happen if libel earned First Amendment protection. Newspapers would be protected, he said, even if they printed such false statements as

> the Secretary of State had given military secrets to the enemy; the Secretary of the Treasury had embezzled public funds; that the Governor of a state poisoned his wife; that the head of the public health service polluted water with germs; that the mayor and city are corrupt.[5]

No Grounds for Upsetting Precedent

According to Nachman, the case did not present any special facts or circumstances that would justify reversing the jury's decision and changing the firmly established law of libel. Nachman demonstrated that in Alabama and throughout the country, juries were given great latitude in awarding damages.

Justice Arthur J. Goldberg questioned what part of the advertisement referred to Commissioner Sullivan. The third and sixth paragraphs of the advertisement had been called objectionable throughout the trial. These two paragraphs were the heart of the case. Nachman answered Justice Goldberg by saying that paragraphs three and six related to the conduct of the police and therefore were about the commissioner.

> Justice Goldberg: How about the padlocking of the door?

Nachman: Yes, Sir. That is a typical sort of police action.

Justice Goldberg: Does "state authorities" mean police?

Nachman: The jury could reason that the municipal police are "state authorities."

He explained to the Court why the advertisement was "of and concerning" the police commissioner. "We don't think that the advertisement has to say 'The police arrest . . .' in order to contend that 'arrest' refers to the police. A normal intelligent reader understands that arrests are made by the police."

Nachman told the justices that under the law, a newspaper could not publish a "malicious lie about a public official." This "would be a brand new page in our jurisprudence," and have "a devastating effect on our civilization."[6] He contended that the Supreme Court had never distinguished libel cases in terms of public officials and private citizens.

Truth as a Defense

When a plaintiff sues a defendant in court, he or she begins by filing a written complaint. The complaint has a numbered list of the violations he believes the defendant has committed. The defendant then files an answer to the complaint. The answer contains numbered responses to the plaintiff's complaint. In the answer, the defendant can list "defenses," that is, a list of reasons why the plaintiff should not win the case. One of the defenses available to a newspaper at a libel trial is truth. If a newspaper proves that the writing about the public figure is true, then the jury has an opportunity to weigh that fact against the complaint by the plaintiff. A public figure cannot claim that his reputation has been damaged by the truth. The statement about the person must be false in order for it to be deemed libelous.

At the trial in Alabama, *The New York Times* had not argued that the facts of the "Heed Their Rising Voices" advertisement were true. In fact, they agreed that some of the statements were false, such as those concerning the song the students had sung and the reason some students were expelled.[7]

At the oral argument, the justices questioned Nachman about this issue. Justice William O. Douglas asked whether at the trial the jury had been asked to decide whether the advertisement was true or false. Nachman explained that *The New York Times* had not raised the truth of the advertisement in its defense. Since the *Times* did not raise the defense of truth, the law of Alabama required the jurors to conclude that the advertisement was false.[8] Nachman also said that the ad was "completely false, and there was no attempt by the *Times* to say that any of it was true."[9]

The New York Times had lost an opportunity to mitigate damages. Mitigating damages is a legal term, which is a chance to do something to correct the harm done to the plaintiff.

At the time the advertisement was published, the governor of Alabama had demanded a retraction. The *Times* complied. Commissioner Sullivan also asked the paper to print a retraction, but the *Times* did not do so. If the newspaper prints a retraction, the successful plaintiff cannot claim punitive damages. Rather, the libeled person can recover only the actual damages, or amount of money he lost as a result of the publication. Actual damages can be the amount of a person's salary if

African-American students at Alabama State University talk with a reporter in 1960. Protests on campus formed the basis for the "Heed Their Rising Voices" advertisement.

he loses his job as a result of the defamation. If the *Times* had printed a retraction for Commissioner Sullivan, Sullivan would not have been allowed to win the $500,000. Since the *Times* did not publish a retraction, Sullivan was entitled to punitive damages, the lower court had ruled.

Nachman summarized this point for the court at oral argument. He stated that the laws of Alabama offered several ways to accommodate the First Amendment freedom of speech and press. Alabama had a retraction statute that the *Times* refused to exercise. Alabama law offers truth as an absolute defense to a libel action. Alabama law also offers "fair comment," the opportunity for a public official to respond to the published statement. Nachman said that since the *Times* had elected neither of these options, the jury's award of $500,000 in punitive damages was proper.

Waiting for a Decision

Once all the briefs were filed and oral argument was heard, the parties had to wait for the Court to render its decision. The nine justices of the Supreme Court would have conferences to discuss the case and the law and precedent on the issues. They would review the law with each other, vote, and write one or more opinions of the case.

chapter 7

The Supreme Court Rules

Three months after the lawyers for Sullivan and *The New York Times* made their arguments, the Supreme Court handed down its decision. The nine justices unanimously agreed with *The New York Times*. It reversed the decision of the Supreme Court of Alabama and took away the $500,000 award from Commissioner Sullivan. Most significantly, the Court brought libel within the protection of the First Amendment.

"We hold that the rule of law applied by the Alabama courts is constitutionally deficient for failure to provide the safeguards for freedom of speech and of the press."[1] The opinion was fifty-one pages long and defined what Wechsler had called in his brief for *The New York Times* "the central meaning of the First Amendment."[2]

The Majority Opinion

Justice William Brennan wrote the majority opinion for the Court. Justice Brennan served on the United States Supreme Court for thirty-four years (1956–1990) and left a legacy of supporting individual freedoms. He once said that he believed that the Constitution existed to guarantee the "essential dignity and worth of each individual."[3]

William Joseph Brennan, Jr., was born in Newark, New Jersey, on April 25, 1906. The son of Irish immigrants, he was the second of eight children. His father was a furnace operator at Ballantine Brewery in Newark and a union leader. Brennan graduated from the University of Pennsylvania's Wharton School of Finance and Harvard Law School.

Brennan practiced law in New Jersey, specializing in labor relations and helping unions and management to settle their disputes. Brennan served in the Army during World War II. Upon his return to New Jersey after the war, Brennan worked to reform the New Jersey court system. He became a state court judge in 1949 and was appointed to the New Jersey Supreme Court in 1952. President Dwight D. Eisenhower appointed Brennan to the United States Supreme Court in 1956.

Brennan began the opinion with a review of the facts of the case. At the original trial, the appeal, and before the Supreme Court, *The New York Times* had pressed the argument that the advertisement did not mention the police commissioner. The newspaper repeatedly questioned how Sullivan could expect to win a libel case when the advertisement of which he complained was not about him. The Court agreed with *The New York Times*. It held that there was not enough evidence to connect the statements in the advertisement with the commissioner individually.[4]

Brennan read the two paragraphs of the advertisement, paragraphs three and six, that had been the basis for the commissioner's lawsuit. He reviewed the factual errors in the advertisement. He described the retraction that the *Times* had printed for Governor Patterson of Alabama, but not for Commissioner Sullivan. Finally, he wrote about the trial and the way the judge had instructed the jury. He acknowledged that the jury had been told about libel *per se*. "The [Alabama] law implies legal injury from the bare fact of publication itself . . . falsity and malice are presumed."[5]

Then, in decisive language, he wrote a new page in First Amendment law:

> We reverse the judgment. We hold that the rule of law applied by the Alabama courts is constitutionally

deficient for failure to provide the safeguards for freedom of speech and of the press that are required by the First . . . Amendment.[6]

Justice Brennan wrote that the case presented an issue that the United States Supreme Court had never previously decided. This was the first time the Court had ever been asked to determine whether a public official, unlike a private citizen, could claim to be libeled. Likewise, this was the first time a publication asked the Court to extend First Amendment protection to its words and criticism of public officials. There was no precedent for this precise issue. As Justice Goldberg wrote in his concurring opinion in the case, "We must recognize that we are writing upon a clean slate."[7]

The Central Meaning of the First Amendment

Justice Brennan reviewed the nation's history and commitment to the freedom of speech and the press. He harkened back to James Madison and the importance of a government by the people. The First Amendment ensured that Americans had a chance to voice their opinions. The leaders of government would then have a chance to hear and to respond to the people. The First Amendment allows unrestricted exchange of ideas to help bring about the political and social changes that the people want. It reflected a "profound national commitment to the principle that debate on public issues should be uninhibited, robust, and wide open."[8]

One of the pitfalls of this commitment to free debate was the possibility of errors. Americans accept this risk for the greater good of the ability to speak and publish freely. Justice Brennan accepted the fact that in order for the First Amendment freedoms to thrive, the speaker needs breathing space. This is especially important when the speaker wants to criticize the government. A speaker or writer has to have the license or breathing space to voice opinions without fear of being sued.[9]

He acknowledged that truth as a defense to a libel action was not enough to afford people their freedom of speech and press. If the critic of the public official had to be able to prove the truth of all his statements, he might be reluctant to speak. He may doubt that the truth could be proven with certainty in court, or he may worry that it would cost a great deal of money to do so. People, afraid of libel, tend to control their speech to make sure it stays clear of the unlawful libelous speech and publication, he noted. The result, for Brennan, was that the current rule of libel "dampens the vigor and limits the variety of public debate."[10]

Libel Gains First Amendment Protection

In *New York Times* v. *Sullivan*, the Supreme Court created a new class of protected speech. It now included libel in the class of speech that is entitled to First Amendment protection. Justice Brennan noted, "Although the Sedition Act was never tested in this Court, the attack upon its validity has carried the day in the court of history." He pointed out that because the Sedition Act restrained people from criticizing the government, it violated the First Amendment. He wrote that the importance of the freedom of the press is especially apparent at times when the country has a crisis that divided the country, such as a war or the civil rights movement. He also noted that speech

> may well include vehement, caustic, and sometimes unpleasantly sharp attacks on government and public officials. The present advertisement, as an expression of grievance and protest on one of the major public issues of our time, would seem clearly to qualify for the constitutional protection.[11]

Because of this ruling, a public official can no longer sue to collect a money judgment for the defamatory false statements made about his public conduct. The Court relied on the case of *Barr* v. *Matteo*, which gave immunity to the public officials. Public officials are immune from libel for statements made in the exercise of their public duties.

They are given immunity to allow them to perform their public jobs freely and uninhibited by fear of lawsuits. The Court then made a logical extension of the *Barr* v. *Matteo* immunity principle. If the public official is immune from libelous statements he makes, members of the public must have the same immunity in the statements they make about the public official. Brennan wrote that it is as much the citizen's duty to criticize the official as it is the official's duty to administer the government.[12] To allow otherwise would give the public officials "an unjustified preference over the public they serve" if the people did not enjoy the same immunity.[13]

The Court then found that the advertisement was not "of and concerning" Commissioner Sullivan. The justices reviewed the evidence from the trial that was presented in *The New York Times*'s and Sullivan's briefs. They noted that the advertisement did not refer to Sullivan, either by name or official position. The statements in the advertisement presented no basis for the belief that it attacked Commissioner Sullivan. They concluded that the jury assumed without specific testimony or evidence that because of his official position, he must have been attacked in the advertisement.[14]

Actual Malice

The Court decided that libel *per se* was inappropriate because of the person's status as a public official.

The case created the actual-malice standard. This means that a public official must prove that the publisher or speaker knew that the information published was false. Factual errors (naming the wrong song, number of arrests, reasons for arrests) did not warrant damages to the libeled public official. The Court concluded that *The New York Times* had not acted with actual malice. Justice Brennan reviewed the steps the newspaper had taken prior to the publication. Their Advertising Acceptability Department had accepted a letter from the Committee to Defend Dr. Martin Luther King and the Struggle for Freedom in the South. The letter certified that the committee had the permission of all the sixty-four people who signed the advertisement. The Court was satisfied that the *Times* advertising department neither knew that several facts stated in the advertisement were false nor disregarded their falsehood.

Concurring Opinions

Two justices, Hugo Black and Arthur Goldberg, wrote concurring opinions in *New York Times* v. *Sullivan*. Justice Douglas joined each of the concurring opinions, marking his agreement with the specific points of each concurrence. Justice Black agreed with the Court's overall conclusion to reverse the Alabama Supreme Court. He wanted the Court to go even further. He thought

One of the arguments made by Sullivan's attorneys was that the ad constituted libel because it claimed that students were expelled for leading a demonstration at the capitol. In actuality, they were expelled for conducting a sit-in, like these protesters in Virginia in 1960.

the newspaper had an "absolute, unconditional constitutional right" to publish the advertisement that criticized the government. He did not want the Court to impose the actual-malice standard. He thought that malice, a state of mind, would be difficult to prove in court.[15]

Justice Black also thought that the $500,000

jury award showed that the American press was in financial danger. If enough people brought such libel lawsuits, newspapers could be run out of business. Black stated:

> This Nation, I suspect, can live in peace without libel suits based on public discussions of public affairs and public officials. But I doubt that a country can live in freedom where its people can be made to suffer physically or financially for criticizing their government, its actions, or its officials.[16]

Justice Goldberg also agreed with the decision of the Court. Separately, he wrote that the freedom of the press is an absolute guarantee. Like Justice Black, Justice Goldberg thought the Court's ruling could have been even more protective of the freedom of the press. He was concerned that if public criticism of the government could be found libelous, then it could be silenced.

Public Officials Are Held to a Higher Standard

Brennan showed an important difference between the *Sullivan* case and the many libel cases that had reached the Supreme Court before it. *Sullivan* was different because the person complaining of libel was a public official. The people of Montgomery had elected him to his office. The Court recognized for the first time that the press needed some breathing room to criticize officials of the government.

The results of *New York Times* v. *Sullivan* are several:

◇ The press now has breathing space, or the "right to be wrong," as long as it acts neither recklessly nor maliciously. It does not have to worry that the slightest factual errors will trigger lawsuits and judgments that would put the newspaper in bankruptcy or out of business.[17]

◇ The decision played an important part in the civil rights movement through the 1960s, after the decision came down from the Supreme Court. After *The New York Times* won the case, it and other newspapers continued to report on racism, civil rights activists, and social change. With national exposure through the national press, the momentum for new laws increased.

◇ The decision has helped the news media to become a major political force in America in the last forty years. Investigative journalism has thrived since *New York Times* v. *Sullivan*. Major events—such as Watergate, the Vietnam War, the war in the Persian Gulf, and the attacks of September 11, 2001—have all been covered thoroughly by journalists.

chapter 8

Freedom of The Press After New York Times v. Sullivan and Today

The Supreme Court's landmark First Amendment case of *New York Times* v. *Sullivan* changed the course of libel lawsuits for public officials. It became much more difficult for a public official to win a libel lawsuit against a publisher. Before *New York Times* v. *Sullivan*, an official only had to prove that the false, damaging statement was published and was about him. Now, he had to prove that the publisher knew that the information published was false and published it anyway.

Today, the Supreme Court's opinion in *New York Times* v. *Sullivan* is still the law of the land. However, the rule has been extended to apply to people other than public officials. The rule also extends to other public figures.[1] A public figure is someone who is in the public eye because of his job or position. Public figures include athletes; movie, television, and music personalities; famous authors; school officials; and military leaders. However, *false* statements about a public figure are not protected by the First Amendment. A public figure can sue for libel and win if he proves that the speaker, author, or publisher knew the statement to be false. He or she can also win if the speaker, author, or publisher is reckless about the falsehood, such as by failing to investigate or ask about the truth.

Clarifying "Actual Malice"

The Supreme Court reviewed the definition of the actual-malice standard in 1974.[2] A Chicago policeman named Nuccio shot and killed a young man and was convicted of second-degree murder. The man's family sued Nuccio in civil court. Their attorney, Elmer Gertz, was a prominent lawyer. A magazine, *American Opinion*, published an article that falsely stated that Gertz was a Communist and part of a conspiracy to frame the policeman for murder. Gertz sued the magazine for defamation. In its defense, the magazine argued that its publications should be protected by the First Amendment. It said that the rule of *New York Times* v. *Sullivan*, proof of actual malice, should apply to any case where the statement is about a matter of public importance.

The Supreme Court heard the case and ruled that the status of the defamed person, not the nature of the statement, would determine the standard of review. It classified "public officials," "public figures," and "private persons." It pointed out that public officials (such as Commissioner Sullivan) and public figures (such as a movie star or sports figure) have greater access to the media. By virtue of their public positions, they have a better chance to respond to statements that are made against them. A famous person has a better opportunity to get a call to or from a reporter than an ordinary private citizen. They also reasoned that public officials and public figures both expect public scrutiny because of their status. They held that Gertz was neither a public official nor a public figure. Therefore, the First Amendment would not protect the statements.[3]

The *Gertz* case gave the justices the chance to discuss libel as it related to the private citizen. Most states still had libel *per se* as their controlling law. As was the case with Commissioner Sullivan before the Supreme Court ruling, the defamed person did not have to prove anything more than that the published statement was about him. Injury to his reputation was presumed by the mere publication. The *Gertz* case makes an important legal clarification. In a libel case, a private person must prove a publisher's negligence, while a public figure must prove that the publisher acted with actual malice.

The Issue Today

Not all libel lawsuits end with a determination by the United States Supreme Court. In fact, most cases are won or lost in the state trial court. These cases involve classifying the plaintiff as a public official, a public figure, or a private person as well as the issue of actual malice. These issues are debated on a regular basis in state courts around the country.

In October 2003, a libel case was decided in a state court in Minnesota. This case demonstrates the struggle that courts have to this day with the elements of a defamation trial. In the Minnesota case, police officer Thomas Schlieman sued KARE-TV for libel. Officer Schlieman had shot and killed a man, Kevin Hartwig. Schlieman said it was done in self-defense. A television reporter, Dennis Stauffer, said on air that two people who claimed to have witnessed the shooting had said that Hartwig was not being aggressive when he was shot. Schlieman sued both the reporter and the television station for defamation. The jury found that the statements were not defamatory. The police officer appealed and won a new trial.[4] The appellate court ruled that the trial court had given the jury a misstatement of the law of libel. At the new trial, the police officer won and was awarded $110,000. The television station appealed, and it won on appeal. The appellate court found that the police officer did not prove that the news report was made with actual malice. It noted that to show actual malice, Schlieman had to prove that Stauffer and KARE-TV knew the statement was false or that they recklessly disregarded whether the statement was true or false.[5]

In a recent Pennsylvania state court case, a judge sued a newspaper. The paper had falsely reported that the judge released a violent criminal from jail. The newspaper won at trial, because the judge could not prove that the people at the newspaper had acted with actual malice.[6]

In an Ohio case, a judge sued the *Cleveland Plain Dealer* for an editorial that criticized the way the judge had been elected to the bench. The case was dismissed because the publication was a matter of opinion on the editorial page. Additionally, the editor had done significant research on the facts that she included in the editorial. Even though there were mistakes in the editorial, no actual malice could be found.[7]

Internet Libel

The growth of the Internet in recent years has created new issues for the freedom of the press and freedom of speech. As technology advances, the means of publication grow. Historically, each new type of medium brings new challenges to the freedoms of speech and press. In the early days of media, pamphlets were written, printed by hand, and circulated. For instance, in 1776 Thomas Paine wrote *Common Sense*, an anonymous pamphlet that criticized the monarchy and encouraged independence of the colonies. The nineteenth-century news media benefited from the industrial revolution. New machines such as the modernized printing press and typewriter created advances for both news gathering and printing. The telegraph emerged as a means to send information. News agencies developed. Laws over the freedom of the press have adapted to the new forms of media. Just as the laws of libel were tested in newspapers and magazines, so too are they now being tested with respect to Internet publications. After all, a falsehood is no less a falsehood whether it is published in a newspaper, magazine, or on the Internet.

A distinguishing characteristic of the Internet, as opposed to news media and traditional press, is its interactive capability. Compared to traditional news sources, the Supreme Court said, it is a "unique and wholly new medium of worldwide human communication."[8] It allows an unlimited number of voices to speak and to be heard. It stretches across the world. It also allows practically instant access to news.

In 1991, the issue arose of how an Internet service provider can be responsible for a libel that gets posted on the Internet. In *Cubby* v. *CompuServe*, the United States federal district court in New York dealt with this issue.[9] CompuServe is an Internet service provider that hosted an "electronic library." One of the features in the electronic library was a journalism forum. The forum contained electronic bulletin boards, interactive online conferences, and information grouped by topics. One such electronic bulletin board in the journalism forum was "Rumorville USA," a newsletter that provided daily reports about broadcast journalists. CompuServe had no control over the content of "Rumorville USA." The plaintiff, Cubby, Inc., a competitor of Rumorville, alleged that Rumorville published false and defamatory statements about the owners of Cubby, Inc., on the journalism forum. They sued CompuServe for carrying the statements on their service.

The court held that the Internet service provider was similar to a bookstore. A bookstore is a depository of information, but it does not control the content of the books. The Internet is a vast source of information, but the Internet service providers do not control what different users and Web sites post on the Internet. Therefore, since they do not control the content, they cannot be liable for defaming anyone. However, the person who posts a defamatory message can be sued for libel, the court held.[10]

Congress has acted in regulating this area. In 1996, Congress enacted the Communications Decency Act (CDA).[11] The act was intended to balance individual freedoms of expression against the concerns of the community for violence and indecency that is available on the Internet. One purpose of the CDA was to protect online service providers from liability for content that they did not produce. It realized that the Internet does not have editors, as newspapers do. They could not be found responsible for the libel because they are not the true publishers of the statement. Under this law, Internet service providers are immune from lawsuits that are based on information posted by parties that use their service. While the CDA was later struck down, it demonstrates the willingness of Congress to pass laws that do not restrict freedom of speech and press. Several states have passed their own laws following the principles of the CDA.

The Internet service provider does have an obligation to remove defamatory statements once it learns of them. In the case of *Zeran* v. *America Online Inc.*, the courts distinguished between the Internet service provider as a publisher and as a distributor. Under the Communications Decency Act, America Online and other similar Internet

The invention of personal computers and the development of the Internet led to new questions about libel and freedom of the press.

service providers cannot be sued as the publisher of something posted on its service that is libelous. However, when America Online learns of the libel and continues to carry it, it becomes a distributor of libel. Under these circumstances, they can be sued.[12]

People who use the Internet certainly have First Amendment rights. To make a case of libel, a plaintiff still has to make all the proofs that *New York Times* v. *Sullivan* and the cases extended by it require. In cases dealing with public officials or public figures, the plaintiff must prove that the words were published with actual malice. In some ways, though, the issue of the public figure plaintiff is less important in Internet cases because there is no limit to the access to the Internet. Anyone who has the means can use it. Just as a person can defame someone online, so too can the defamed person respond to the alleged defamation. The Internet makes it easier for a person to respond to online statements he thinks are libelous. He does not have to try to get a newspaper reporter to hear him. He can, if he chooses, respond point by point online to what he thinks is defamatory.[13]

Some issues that are likely to be raised by the Internet include the following:

⬦ Will the electronic services (such as America Online and MSN) that make many different newspapers available also be held legally liable for statements made online by the subscribers?

⬦ Should newspapers correct mistaken stories that continue to be available online? If so, should it rewrite the original story, just post a correction to the inaccurate story, or publish a separate correction?

⬦ Since the Internet is in use all over the country and the world, will publishers be able to be sued in all fifty states and in foreign countries?

◇ Several celebrities have brought lawsuits to stop Internet users from posting photographs of them. Does this violate the freedom of the press?

Undoubtedly, the First Amendment issues raised by the use of the Internet will increase as time goes on. The law of libel will continue to grow and to change. Challenges to the First Amendment will continue, and it will persevere. Despite this growth, or perhaps because of this growth, the message of the Founding Fathers and the "central meaning of the First Amendment" will continue to prove itself in the test of time.

chapter 9

Moot Court: Your Turn to Debate

In this chapter, you will learn how to participate in a mock judicial proceeding of your own. One type of court exercise is called "moot court." A moot court is a dramatization of a hypothetical (fictitious) or real case that went before an appeals court or the Supreme Court. The purpose of these courts is to rule on a lower court's decision. It is different from a trial in that no witnesses appear and testify, just as no witnesses are called in a Supreme Court case. Also, the focus is on whether the court below made any mistakes rather than on finding all the facts of a case.

In moot court, the players take the roles of judges, clerks, attorneys, and journalists. They do research, write briefs, and argue legal issues before a make-believe panel of appeals court judges. The exercise hones research, writing, and debate skills.

Taking part in a moot court is a fun way to get a feeling for how a real court case occurs. Try a moot court activity with your class or club. Here's how.[1]

Step 1: Assign Roles

Here are the roles you will need to fill:

- ◇ Judges. If the group is large enough, have nine justices like the Supreme Court has. Otherwise, have a panel of three appellate court judges. Choose one person to be Chief Justice and direct the proceeding. The judges hear the attorneys' arguments, question them, and then write and deliver the final ruling. The court's majority opinion is the position agreed upon by a majority of the panel. Individual judges may choose to issue concurring or dissenting opinions of their own.

- ◇ Two or more court clerks. They work with the judges to prepare five or more questions to ask the attorneys during oral arguments. Judicial clerks also help with research for judges' opinions.

- ◇ A team of two or more attorneys for the appellant. They try to show that the court below was wrong and the opposite ruling should occur.

- ◇ A team of two or more attorneys for the appellee. They believe the court below ruled correctly.

◇ A designated spokesperson to present the argument (though any of the attorneys can answer questions from the judges). Attorneys must address the major issues by presenting the most persuasive arguments for their side.

◇ Two or more reporters. They interview the attorneys before the case and write news stories about the facts of the case and the final ruling.

◇ The bailiff, who calls the court to order. The bailiff will also time each side's oral argument.

Step 2: Prepare Your Case

Part 1: Gather Information

The hypothetical case you will hear and decide is outlined below:

Students at Smalltown Middle School had a car wash, a book sale, and a bake sale to raise money for their school field trip to the National Archives in Washington, D.C. The students of Smalltown couldn't wait to get to the nation's capital, where they would see the original Bill of Rights that the Founding Fathers had enacted and signed. They raised $1,500, which would pay for the whole trip.

To their shock and dismay, however, the money disappeared. Later that week, the town paper, the *Smalltown Gazette*, printed a newspaper article entitled, "Mayor Mooches: Spends $1,500 on Family

Trip to Fun Land." The story stated that it was unknown where Mayor McDougal, who supported his family on the town salary, could have come up with the money for the family vacation. It also stated in the story that "It's a shame our middle school students won't be taking their trip to Washington, D.C. Mr. Mayor, we hope you enjoy your vacation." Later that year, the mayor lost his reelection campaign.

USA Online is an Internet service provider. It hosts Web sites from around the country and the world, and does not review the content of the Web sites. The *Smalltown Gazette.com* carried the story about the mayor's vacation.

The editor of the *Smalltown Gazette*, Percy Paperman, had covered Smalltown for years. He began his career as a beat reporter, and now was running the newspaper. His wife, Pamela Paperman, was also interested in politics, and wanted to run for mayor. In fact, she defeated Mayor McDougal in the election that year.

The mayor of Smalltown demanded a retraction of the story. The paper printed a retraction that stated that the mayor had saved $20 per week for the last year and a half, in order to have enough money to take his family on the vacation. Mayor McDougal also asked USA Online to discontinue hosting the *Smalltown Gazette* story online.

Mayor McDougal sued the *Smalltown Gazette* and USA Online for libel. He alleged that the statements in the article were false, known to be false by the *Gazette*, but were published nonetheless. He alleged that the Internet service provider should have discontinued running the story online, once they learned of the falsehood. Before the trial occurred, the court dismissed the case against the *Smalltown Gazette* and USA Online, indicating that the mayor had not proven the case of libel under the law as set forth in *New York Times* v. *Sullivan*. The mayor appealed the trial court's decision.

Part 2: Write Your Briefs

A legal brief is a written presentation of your argument. Brainstorm with the lawyers on your team. Which arguments are strongest for you? What are your weaknesses?

You may want to divide up arguments for research and writing. If so, be sure to work as a team to put the brief together. Otherwise, your brief may have holes or read poorly.

Each team should consider the following questions in preparation of the case:

1. What are the different issues in the case? Is the petitioner a public official? Has he presented all the elements of a libel case? Did the newspaper have any defenses available to it? What is the effect of the retraction?

2. How can the mayor prove that the newspaper

acted with actual malice? How can the newspaper prove it did not act with actual malice?

3. Competing interests of the parties: Is the mayor's reputation more important than the freedom of speech?

4. What are the arguments for upholding the ruling of _New York Times_ v. _Sullivan_, and requiring proof of actual malice on the part of the publisher?

5. If the court reverses the trial court's decision, it sends the case back to the lower court for a new trial. What instructions or guidance would the court pass on to the lower court to ensure that the case is decided in accordance with the law?

In real life, court rules spell out what briefs must contain. Use these rules for your moot court activity:

1. The cover page should have the case name, _McDougal_ v. _Smalltown Gazette and USA Online_. Say whether it is the case for the Appellant or the Appellee. List the lawyers' names.

2. The text of the brief should have these sections:

   A. Statement of the issue for review: What question is before the court?

   B. Statement of the case: What is this case about? How did the trial court rule?

   C. Statement of the facts: Briefly describe the facts relevant to the case.

D. Summary of the argument: Sum up your argument in 150 words or less.

E. Argument: Spell out the legal arguments that support your side. You can split this into sections with subheadings for each part. Include references to cases or authorities that help your side.

F. Conclusion: Ask the court to rule for your client.

3. Real appeals briefs may be thirty pages long. Limit your brief to no more than five typed pages, double-spaced, or about 1,250 words. If possible, type on a computer. Otherwise, write very neatly.

4. On an agreed date, each team gives the other side a copy of its brief. Each judge gets a copy too. If you do this in class, give the teacher a copy. Be sure each team member keeps a copy of the brief too.

In real life, lawyers often prepare reply briefs. They answer points made by the other side. You won't do that. But you should be ready to answer their points in oral argument.

Part 3: Prepare for Oral Argument

Judges should read all the briefs before oral argument and prepare questions for the lawyers.

Each side will have up to fifteen minutes to argue its case.

Step 3: Hold the Oral Argument

Part 1: Assemble the Participants

◇ The judges sit in a panel at the head of the room. This is the bench. They should not enter until the bailiff calls the court to order. A speaking podium faces the bench.

◇ The appellant's team of attorneys (counsel for the mayor) sits at one side, facing the judges.

◇ The appellee's teams (counsel for the *Smalltown Gazette* and USA Online) sit at the opposite side, also facing the judges.

◇ The reporters sit at the back.

◇ As the judges enter, the bailiff calls the court to order: "Oyez (oy-yay)! Oyez! Oyez! The _____ Court of the United States is now in session with the Honorable Chief Justice _____ presiding. All will stand and remain standing until the judges are seated and the Chief Justice has asked all present to be seated."

Part 2: Present the Case

◇ The Chief Justice calls the case and asks whether the parties are ready. Each team's spokesperson answers, "Yes."

◇ The appellant's spokesperson approaches the podium saying, "May it please the court." Then argument begins. Judges interrupt when they wish to ask a question. The attorneys respectfully answer any questions as asked. Don't get flustered if a judge interrupts with a question. Answer the question honestly. Then move on.

⬦ Then the appellee's team takes its turn.

⬦ Each team has up to fifteen minutes to present its argument. If the appellant wants, it can save five minutes of its time to rebut the appellees' argument. If so, the spokesperson should inform the court before sitting down.

⬦ After the arguments, the bailiff has everyone rise as the judges retire to chambers to debate their decision.

⬦ At this time, reporters may interview lawyers for the parties and begin working on their articles.

⬦ After an agreed-upon time, the judges return and present their ruling, announced by the Chief Justice.

Step 4: Publish and Report

⬦ A few days later, the court issues its majority opinion in written form, along with any dissenting opinions and individual concurring opinions.

⬦ At the same time, the reporters' stories are made available.

Questions for Discussion

1. David Brown was arrested for violating the Sedition Act (see chapter 2). Suppose Brown had appealed his conviction, asserting that his First Amendment rights had been violated. If Brown's case had reached the Supreme Court in the early 1800s, what do you think the outcome would have been?

2. How does the freedom of the press help encourage social change?

3. What if the Supreme Court had denied the petition for certiorari to *The New York Times*? Do you think that the First Amendment would have evolved to where it is today, with an actual-malice standard?

4. In order to prevail in a libel case, a private citizen needs to prove that the publisher was negligent. A public figure has to prove "actual malice." Should a public figure have a different standard for proving libel than a private citizen? Why?

5. If you were a member of the Supreme Court in 1964, would you have voted with the majority (in favor of *The New York Times*) or with the dissent (for Sullivan)? Why?

6. How has the evolution of the Internet affected the freedom of the press? Should the government be allowed to control the content of Internet sites?

Chapter Notes

Chapter 1. The 1960s and the Civil Rights Movement

1. Janus Adams, *Freedom Days: 365 Inspired Moments in Civil Rights History* (New York: John Wiley & Sons, Inc., 1998).
2. Ibid.
3. *The New York Times*, March 29, 1960, p. 25.
4. Ibid., p. 25.
5. Ibid.
6. Anthony Lewis, *Make No Law. The Sullivan Case and the First Amendment* (New York: Random House, 1991), pp. 12–13.
7. *New York Times* v. *Sullivan*, 376 US 254 (1964), Brennan, J. opinion for the majority at fn. 2, and author's inquiry to *The New York Times* advertising department.

Chapter 2. The Founding Fathers and the First Amendment

1. *Congressional Register*, June 8, 1789, vol. 1, p. 427.
2. *Pennsylvania Packet*, December 18, 1787.
3. *Mills v. Alabama*, 384 US 214, 218 (1966).
4. Sedition Act, July 14, 1798, c. 74, 1 Stat. 596.
5. Lester J. Cappon, ed., "Letter to Abigail Adams," *The Adams-Jefferson Letters: The Complete Correspondence Between Thomas Jefferson and Abigail and John Adams* (Chapel Hill: University of North Carolina Press, 1959), pp. 274–276.

Chapter 3. Freedom of the Press: History and Cases

1. *Masses Publishing Co. v. Patten*, 244 Fed. 535 (S.D.N.Y. 1917).
2. *Masses Publishing Co. v. Patten*, 246 Fed. 24 (2d Cir. 1917).
3. *Schenck v. United States*, 249 US 47, 52 (1919).
4. *Debs v. United States*, 249 US 211, 214, (1919).
5. *Abrams v. United States*, 250 US 616 (1919).

6. *Abrams v. United States*, 250 US 616, 629 (1919), Holmes, J. dissenting.

7. William A. Hachten, *The Supreme Court on Freedom of the Press: Decisions and Dissents* (Ames: Iowa State University Press, 1968), p. 41.

8. *Near v. Minnesota*, 283 US 697, 701, (1931), citing Mason's Minnesota Statutes, 1927, 10123–1 to 10123–3.

9. *State ex rel. Floyd B. Olson v. Howard A. Guilford and others*, 179 Minn. 40 (1929).

10. *Chaplinsky v. New Hampshire*, 315 US 568, 571–72 (1942).

11. *Beauharnais v. Illinois*, 343 US 250 (1952).

12. Ill. Rev. Stat., 1949, c. 38 § 471.

13. *Beauharnais* at 253.

14. *Beauharnais v. Illinois*, 343 US 250, 270 (1952), Black, J. dissenting.

Chapter 4. The Road to the Supreme Court

1. Anthony Lewis, *Make No Law: The Sullivan Case and the First Amendment* (New York: Random House, 1991), p. 31.

2. *The New York Times*, March 29, 1960, p. 25.

3. Ibid.

4. Anthony Lewis, *Make No Law. The Sullivan Case and the First Amendment* (New York: Random House, 1991), p. 29.

5. Ibid.

6. *Marbury v. Madison*, 5 US 137 (1803).

7. 28 U.S.C. §1257.

8. Henry Campbell Black, *Black's Law Dictionary*, 5th ed. (St. Paul, Minn.: West Publishing, 1979), p. 766.

9. Rules of the Supreme Court of the United States. R. 10.1

10. Address of Chief Justice Vinson before the American Bar Association, 69 S. Ct. v, vi (1949), September 7, 1949.

11. R. S. Ct. 13.1.

12. "Supreme Court of the United States: The Justices' Caseload," August 23, 2003, <http://www.supremecourtus.gov> (December 1, 2004).

13. Eugene Gressman, *Much Ado About Certiorari*, 52 Geo. L.J. 742 (1964).

14. Lewis, pp. 105–107.

15. R. S. Ct. 15.2.

16. Lewis, p. 111.

17. R. S. Ct. 16.

Chapter 5. The Case for *The New York Times*

1. Philip B. Kurland and Gerhard Casper, eds., *Landmark Briefs and Arguments of the Supreme Court of the United States: Constitutional Law* (Arlington, Va.: University Publications of America, 1975), p. 405, transcribing Petitioner New York Times Company's "Brief for the Petitioner" in no. 39, p. 2.

2. *Roth v. United States*, 354 US 476, 484 (1957).

3. Kurland and Casper, pp. 29–30.

4. Ibid., p. 49.

5. *Cantwell v. Connecticut* 310 US 296 (1940).

6. Henry Campbell Black, *Black's Law Dictionary*, 5th ed. (St. Paul, Minn.: West Publishing Company, 1979), p.171.

7. *Cantwell v. Connecticut*, 310 US 296 (1940).

8. *Barr v. Matteo*, 360 US 564, 575 (1959).

9. Kurland and Casper, p. 456, "Brief for the Petitioner," p. 53.

10. Richard N. Winfield, *New York Times v. Sullivan: The Next Twenty Years* (New York: Practicing Law Institute, 1984), p. 60.

11. Black, p. 863.

12. Kurland and Casper, pp. 457, 54.

13. Recording of the oral argument before the United States Supreme Court in *New York Times v. Sullivan*, no. 39, January 6, 1964, <http://www.oyez.org/oyez/resource/case/277/> (October 12, 2003).

14. Winfield, p. 58.

15. Kurland and Casper, *supra*, p. 471, transcribing petitioner's brief, p. 68.

16. Recording of the oral argument before the United States Supreme Court in *New York Times v. Sullivan*, no. 39, January 6, 1964, <http://www.oyez.org/oyez/resource/case/277/> (October 12, 2003).

Chapter 6. The Case for Commissioner Sullivan

1. *The New York Times*, March 29, 1960, p. 25.

2. Philip B. Kurland and Gerhard Casper, eds., *Landmark Briefs and Arguments of the Supreme Court of the United States: Constitutional Law* (Arlington, Va.: University Publications of America, 1975), p. 525, transcribing Respondent L.B. Sullivan's "Brief for the Respondent" in no. 39, p. 22.

3. *New York Times* v. *Sullivan*, 376 US 254, 265 (1964).

4. Alabama Code, Title 7, § 914.

5. Kurland and Casper, pp. 525, 22.

6. Recording of the oral argument before the United States Supreme Court in *New York Times* v. *Sullivan*, no. 39, January 6, 1964, <http://www.oyez.org/oyez/resource/case/277/> (October 12, 2003).

7. Kurland and Casper, pp. 532, 29.

8. Richard N. Winfield, *New York Times* v. *Sullivan: The Next Twenty Years* (New York: Practicing Law Institute, 1984), p. 59.

9. Anthony Lewis, *Make No Law. The Sullivan Case and the First Amendment* (New York: Random House, 1991), p. 135.

Chapter 7. The Supreme Court Rules

1. *New York Times* v. *Sullivan*, 376 US 254, 264 (1964).

2. *New York Times* v. *Sullivan*, 376 US 254, 273 (1964).

3. Linda Greenhouse, "William Brennan, 91, Dies, Gave Court Liberal Vision," *The New York Times*, July 25, 1997, p. 1.

4. 376 US 254, 292 (1964).

5. 376 US 254, 262.

6. 376 US 254, 264.

7. 376 US 254, 299.

8. 376 US 254, 269, relying on *Roth* v. *United States*, 354 US 476 (1957).

9. 376 US 254, 271–2, relying on *N.A.A.C.P.* v. *Button*, 371 US 415 (1963).

10. 376 US 254, 279, referencing *Speiser* v. *Randall*, 357 US 526 (1958).

11. 376 US 254, 270.

12. 376 US 254, 282.

13. 376 US 254, 289.

14. 376 US 254, 271.

15. 376 US 254, 293–4.

16. 376 US 254, 297.

17. Tony Mauro, *Illustrated Great Decisions of the Supreme Court* (Washington, D.C.: Congressional Quarterly Press, 2000), p. 132.

Chapter 8. Freedom of the Press After *New York Times* v. *Sullivan* and Today

1. *Curtis Publishing Co.* v. *Butts*, 388 US 130 (1967).

2. *Gertz* v. *Robert Welch, Inc.*, 418 US 323 (1974).

3. Ibid., pp. 343–346.

4. *Schlieman* v. *Gannett Minn. Broad., Inc.*, 637 N.W.2d 297, 2001.

5. Associated Press, "Defamation verdict against TV station overturned," October 28, 2003.

6. *Lewis* v. *Phila. Newspapers, Inc.*, 2003 PA Super 350 (Superior Court of Pennsylvania 2003).

7. *Sikora* v. *Plain Dealer Publ. Co.*, 2003 Ohio 3218 (2003).

8. *Reno* v. *ACLU*, 521 US 844 (1997).

9. *Cubby* v. *CompuServe*, 776 F. Supp. 135 (S.D.N.Y. 1991).

10. Madeleine Schachter, *Law of Internet Speech* (Durham, N.C.: Carolina Academic Press, 2001), p. 198.

11. 47 USCS § 230 (2003).

12. *Zeran* v. *America Online, Inc.*, 129 F.3d 327 (4th Cir. 1997).

13. Mike Godwin, *Cyber Rights: Defending Free Speech in the Digital Age* (Cambridge, Mass.: MIT Press, 2003), p. 89.

Chapter 9. Moot Court: Your Turn to Debate

1. Adapted from Millie Aulbur, "Constitutional Issues and Teenagers," *The Missouri Bar*, n.d., <http://www. mobar.org/teach/clesson.htm> (December 10, 2004); Street Law, Inc., and The Supreme Court Historical Society, "Moot Court Activity," 2002, <http://www.landmarkcases.org/mootcourt. html> (December 10, 2004); with suggestions from Ron Fridell and Kathiann M. Kowalski.

Glossary

defamation—A false, significant statement that injures the reputation of the person about whom the statement is said or written.

freedom of the press—Freedom to publish anything that is true. Americans are guaranteed this liberty in the First Amendment of the United States Constitution.

journalism—The collection, writing, editing, and presentation of news and news articles.

libel—A false publication in writing, printing, or pictures that maliciously damages a person's reputation.

malice—Intent to cause harm.

prior restraint—Stopping speech before it is spoken or published.

retraction—A statement published by a newspaper or other media to "take back" something that was previously published.

seditious libel—A statement or writing that incites rebellion or an image that maliciously damages a leader's reputation.

slander—Defamation by spoken words, rather than writing.

Further Reading

Books

Burns, Kate. *Fighters Against Censorship*. San Diego, Calif.: Lucent Books, 2004.

Egendorf, Laura K., ed. *Should There Be Limits to Free Speech?* San Diego, Calif.: Greenhaven Press, 2003.

Kennedy, Sheila Suess, ed. *Free Expression in America: A Documentary History*. Westport, Conn.: Greenwood Press, 1999.

Levy, Beth, and Denise M. Bonilla, eds. *The Power of the Press*. New York: H.W. Wilson, 1999.

Lively, Donald E. *Landmark Supreme Court Cases: A Reference Guide*. Westport, Conn.: Greenwood Press, 1999.

Nardo, Don. *The Bill of Rights*. San Diego, Calif.: Greenhaven Press, 1998.

Pendergast, Tom, Sara Pendergast, and John Sousanis. *Constitutional Amendments: From Freedom of Speech to Flag Burning*. Detroit, Mich.: UXL, 2001.

Internet Addresses

Supreme Court of the United States
<http://www.supremecourtus.gov>

First Amendment Center
<http://www.firstamendmentcenter.org>

National Constitution Center
<http://www.constitutioncenter.org>

Index